DATE DUE

GAYLORD   PRINTED IN U.S.A.

WILD HORSES

Tom Jackson

Grolier
an imprint of

www.scholastic.com/librarypublishing

Published 2008 by Grolier
An imprint of Scholastic Library Publishing
Old Sherman Turnpike, Danbury,
Connecticut 06816

For The Brown Reference Group plc
Project Editor: Jolyon Goddard
Copy-editors: Lesley Ellis, Lisa Hughes,
    Wendy Horobin
Picture Researcher: Clare Newman
Designers: Jeni Child, Lynne Ross,
    Sarah Williams
Managing Editor: Bridget Giles

Volume ISBN-13: 978-0-7172-6265-6
Volume ISBN-10: 0-7172-6265-0

**Library of Congress
Cataloging-in-Publication Data**

Nature's children. Set 2.
    p. cm.
  Includes bibliographical references and
index.
  ISBN-13: 978-0-7172-8081-0
  ISBN-10: 0-7172-8081-0
  1. Animals--Encyclopedias, Juvenile. I.
Grolier (Firm)
  QL49.N383 2007
  590--dc22
                    2007026928

Printed and bound in China

PICTURE CREDITS

Front Cover: **Shutterstock**: Jeanne Hatch.

Back Cover: **Nature PL**: Shattil and
Rozinski, Lynn M. Stone, Carol Walker;
Superstock: Age Fotostock.

Corbis: Pierre Perrin/Sygma 14, 17; **FLPA**:
Yva Momatiuk/Minden Pictures 41; **Nature
PL**: Geoff Simpson 6; **Photos.com**: 4, 30, 33;
Shutterstock: Robert Broadhead 42,
Winthrop Brookhouse 2–3, 5, 29, 45, 46,
Mary E. Cioffi 10, Mostoryi Sergii Igorevich
34, Denis Pepin 18, Photooiasson 13, Tudor
Stanica 26–27; **Still Pictures**: BIOS/Klein
and Hubert 9, 21, 22, 37, 38.

Contents

FACT FILE: Wild Horses

Class	Mammals (Mammalia)
Order	Odd-toed hoofed mammals (Perissodactyla)
Family	Horse family (Equidae)
Genus	Horses, zebras, and asses (*Equus*)
Species	Domestic and feral horses (*Equus caballus*)
World distribution	Wild horses now live on every continent except Antarctica; in North America wild horses are called mustangs
Habitat	Woodlands, swamps, deserts, grasslands, and mountains
Distinctive physical characteristics	Wild horses are smaller than most domestic horses; they often have a dark stripe on their back, and dark lower legs
Habits	Wild horses live in bands and tend to stay away from people
Diet	Grasses, shrubs, roots, and twigs

Introduction

Some horses live in the wild. They never meet people or set foot inside a stable. Wild horses live all over the world. In North America wild horses are called **mustangs**. The word *mustang* comes from the Spanish word for "stray." In 1900 there were about 2 million mustangs roaming free in the United States. Their numbers have declined, and today there are about 25,000 of them left. However, these small horses are now protected by law.

A wild horse grazes with its young.

A Przewalski's horse stops and looks around.

The Horse Family

Horses are the most common members of a larger family of hoofed **mammals**. This family also contains a number of horselike **species**, such as zebras, donkeys, and a very rare animal called Przewalski's (PRIS-VAAL-SKIS) horse. This horse lives on the grasslands of Mongolia in Asia.

The **domestic horse** is not a natural species. Today's domestic horses look the way they do because they have been bred to look that way over many centuries. Wild horses, other than Przewalski's horse, are domestic horses that have returned to the wild, or become **feral**. Biologists, scientists who study living things, think that all horses are descended from **ancestors**, similar to Przewalski's horse, that were captured by people about 4,000 years ago.

All members of the horse family have a long face, a mane of hair running down their neck, and very long legs that end in a single wide **hoof**.

Ancient Relatives

The horse family has existed for longer than most other types of mammals. Horselike animals were living 60 million years ago—that is, soon after the dinosaurs died out. The ancestors of most other hoofed mammals, such as cattle and deer, appeared much later. The horse family has only a few distant relatives. Those include the rhinoceros and the tapir. Scientists know that rhinoceroses and tapirs are related to horses because most hoofed mammals have an even number of toes. However, horses, tapirs, and rhinoceroses have an odd number of toes.

The first horse species—named the dawn horse—was much smaller than modern members of the family. It was about the size of an adult fox and lived in North America. But like a modern horse it ate leaves and grasses. The dawn horse had four toes covered in a pad of flesh. A modern horse has just a single hard hoof on each of its four feet.

A young mustang learns to gallop.

A mustang rests in the dry plains of Nevada.

Back to America

The modern horse **evolved** in North America about 3 million years ago. These horses roamed across the continent. At one time, North America was connected to Asia by a thin strip of land. The horses crossed this land bridge to Asia. They soon spread throughout Asia and Europe. But about 10,000 years ago all of North America's horses died out. Scientists are not sure exactly why horses disappeared from North America. It might have been due to a change in climate or due to humans, who arrived in North America about that time.

Today's mustangs of North America are descended from European domestic horses that were first brought to America by Spanish explorers about 400 years ago. More horses arrived in North America with later settlers, and soon many had escaped to become feral.

Mustang Country

Horses need a lot of space. There are only a few wild places left in North America that are large enough and open enough to make a good home for wild horses. Most mustangs live in the deserts of Nevada. Horses do not prefer this dry region. Unfortunately, cities and farms take up most of the space in other more suitable **habitats** though.

There are also mustangs in the Pryor Mountains of Montana and Wyoming. Up there mustangs enjoy cooler weather and there is plenty of water for meadows and woodlands to grow among the rugged hills.

All mustangs are shy creatures. Out in the open, Nevada's mustangs gallop away if people get too close. In the Pryor Mountains there are plenty of bushes to hide among. Hidden among the bushes, the curious horses are able to observe people without being noticed. Sometimes they even follow people. But once spotted the mustangs quickly disappear.

Finding food can be hard work for wild horses.

A mother and her young brave the wind on Sable Island.

On Sable Island

Wild horses are adaptable creatures. They can change to suit their surroundings. They survive in the deserts of Nevada and the canyons of Wyoming. They also range on a sandbank on the coast of the North Atlantic.

Sable Island lies off the coast of Nova Scotia, Canada. It is home to 300 wild horses. They share the island with seagulls and seals. Also frequenting the island every year are thousands of Ipswich sparrows that fly from the Deep South to lay their eggs among the grassy sand dunes.

A few people live on the island in order to run the lighthouses. Despite their efforts, the island's shore is still littered with the wrecks of ships that have run aground. Wild horses grazing alongside wrecked ships and sea animals is a most unusual and surprising sight.

Sunshine and Snow

The wild horses of Sable Island live on a beach. In summer the horses enjoy nice weather and plenty of food. In winter it is a different story. With few places to take shelter, the horses endure the full force of the wintery storms that come off the ocean. The horses huddle behind sand dunes to escape the wind and blizzards. They grow a thick coat to keep warm in the freezing temperatures.

During the coldest weeks, the horses use their hooves and powerful legs to break through ice in order to drink from streams. They also must dig in the snow to find grass to eat.

As the tide comes in,
wild horses graze on the
sand at Sable Island.

This domestic horse is drinking melted snow.

Hands Up

Horses raised in the wild are generally smaller than domestic horses. That is because wild horses must survive by eating whatever food they can find. Often they go hungry because there isn't enough food for them. Domestic horses are fed every day by their owners. They are given good food and kept warm and dry in a stable. When they get sick, a veterinarian— a doctor for animals—gives them medicine to help them recover. All this help allows the domestic horses to grow more quickly.

Horses are measured in hands. One hand is 4 inches (10 cm)—the width of an adult's hand. Most wild horses are between 12 and 14 hands. That means the distance from the ground to the animal's shoulder is between 48 and 56 inches (122–142 cm). Most domestic horses are between 14 and 18 hands. Domestic horse breeds that are less than 14.2 hands are called ponies. The biggest horses, called draft horses, can grow to more than 20 hands tall.

Coats and Hats

Wild horses have a variety of coat colors, including brown, gray, white, and black. Today's wild horses have more markings on their body than their domestic cousins. For example, most mustangs have a dark line that runs along the back from the mane to the tail. Sometimes wild horses have faint stripes on their back, a little like the markings on a zebra. The horse's stripes are called "fingermarks."

Native Americans had never seen horses until the European settlers brought them to North America. Some Native Americans quickly learned to catch and ride mustangs. The Cheyenne preferred to ride Medicine Hat mustangs. These horses had a white coat with dark markings on their head and chest. The Cheyenne thought these markings were magical and would protect the rider in battles.

This wild horse's back is clearly marked with the signature dark line.

As this wild horse looks for food in the snow, its long mane falls in its eyes.

22

Horse Hair

A wild horse's hair is its first line of defense against the outside world. Like most other mammals, the hair keeps the animal warm. Wild horses that live in cold places grow a thick, shaggy coat in winter to provide extra warmth. In spring and summer the weather gets warmer. A long coat is then too hot for the horse, so it falls out. This process is called **molting**. The longer hair is replaced with short hair, which is all a horse needs in summer.

The long tail hair and mane never molt. They stay long all year round. In summer the mustangs are often attacked by biting insects. Fortunately, the horse's swishing tail makes an excellent fly swatter.

Pride in Grooming

Wild horses like to keep their coat clean. If they fail to swish any insects off their body with their tail, then the muscles under their skin twitch. This twitching startles the insects and they then fly away. Some insects still manage to bite, causing annoying, even painful itches. Sometimes a horse gets an itch it cannot scratch with its own hooves. It will then rub its back against a tree or roll in the dust to scratch its itching bite.

Wild horses help one another scratch those difficult spots that they cannot reach on their own. Friendly horses often nibble and lick one another to clean away the dirt from matted fur and stop any itches. Two horses often groom each other at the same time. They start at their necks and move along each other's back.

Band Leader

Wild horses live in groups called **bands**. A band does not have an equal number of males and females. In fact, each band has just one adult male, or **stallion**. The other members are females, or **mares**, and their young. The mares form the stallion's **harem**—a group of females who breed with just one male. Most stallions do not have a harem. They live alone or in small bands. They wait for a chance to take over another stallion's harem.

Every horse knows its place in the band. The stallion is the leader. Second in command is a chief mare. All other adult mares have a rank. Even the **foals**, or young horses, have a strict position. A higher-ranking horse always keeps the band members below it in their place. A mustang might jump rank by not waiting for its turn to eat when the band finds a new area to graze. A higher-ranking mustang warns the lower-ranking horse by holding its ears back and tossing its head. If the other horse does not remember its rank, it might get bitten or kicked!

25

A band of mountain mustangs stops and grazes by a stream.

Silent Watchers

Horses have very large eyes. Their large size enables them to gather a lot of light, which means a horse can see almost as well at night as it can in the day. Unlike a person's eyes, which both look forward, a horse's eyes look to the sides. In fact, a horse can see almost all the way around itself. It can even see what is happening behind it. That is a very useful skill since most horses live in wide open grasslands, where danger can strike from any direction.

When they move up and down, or to the left and right, a person's eyes move together. A horse can move its eyes in different directions at the same time. That allows the horse to watch its foal and scan the horizon for danger at the same time.

A young wild horse keeps a close watch on what's going on around it.

Horses have an
excellent sense
of smell.

Sniffing the Wind

Horses have an excellent sense of smell. Their long faces are nearly all nose! The large nostrils lead to a space inside the horse's nose called the nasal cavity. This cavity has a lining that is sensitive to thousands of different odors. A horse can smell things that are far too faint for people to detect. It often sniffs the wind to check what smells are nearby. It can even smell water from miles away.

Like its eyes, each of the horse's pointed ears can move independently of the other. The horse twists each ear around scanning the area for noises, such as the neigh of a friend or the sound of a **predator**.

Wild horses are very shy. If he sees, hears, or smells anything unusual, the stallion will send his band galloping away. He brings up the rear in case he needs to defend his band. Once the band has reached a safe distance, they stop and turn around to take a look at the threat.

Whinny or Neigh?

Wild horses produce a mixture of whinnies, neighs, and snorts to let other members of the band know where they are. When warning the other members of their band that danger is approaching, they produce a louder, more high-pitched cry.

Horses also communicate silently using parts of their body. An angry horse presses its ears back against its head. If you see a horse do this, it is best to stay away from it. If a wild horse suddenly points its ears straight up, it has heard something it doesn't like. Its ears are listening for danger and it is probably frightened.

This wild horse has heard a sound that could mean danger.

These horses are grazing on grass, which is one of their favorite foods.

Time to Chew

Horses are plant eaters. They prefer to eat grass or young leaves from bushes and trees. However, they will eat whatever is available during hard times. In winter Sable Island horses eat seaweed washed up on the shore. The mustangs that live in Nevada eat thorny bushes and dig into the ground for sweet roots when it is cold.

Plant food is tough to eat and it is difficult to get much nutrition out of it. Horses' stomachs don't work as well as the stomachs of other plant eaters, such as cattle or deer. Therefore, horses must chew their food for a long time before it is soft and mushy enough to swallow. Chewing breaks up the plant's fibers, making the food easier to digest. A horse eats about 30 pounds (14 kg) of grass a day, and it spends half the day chewing it!

Tough Hooves

A horse's tough hoof is made from keratin, the same strong material that is in claws, hairs, and fingernails.

The dawn horse had four toes, but today's horses have just one. A horse's hoof is a single huge fingernail that protects that single toe. The hoof grows slowly, just like a fingernail, and so it never gets too worn down by the rough ground.

Domestic horses are fitted with iron horse shoes. That is because domestic horses walk on hard roads, pulling carts, and carrying heavy riders. Without shoes, the horse's hooves would wear away faster than they could grow back.

Strong hooves help this wild horse run on rough ground.

A mustang runs
away from danger
very quickly.

Built for Speed

Horses are expert runners. They needed to be in order to keep out of danger on the grasslands where they evolved. Out there they could be attacked from any direction at any time. The only defense they had was to run away before any attacker could pounce. Today wild horses live in habitats where there is less danger, but the horses still love to run.

Horses have very long legs. Their long single toes make their legs even longer. That allows horses to cover a large distance with each stride. It takes a lot of breath to power the horse's body at high speed. The horse can flare its nostrils very wide to allow more air into its lungs.

Stay Away!

Wild horses **mate** in spring. A stallion will mate with all the mares in his harem. He will make sure that no other stallion breeds with them as well. When a mare is ready to mate she releases a special odor. That odor attracts the stallion from her band. But it also attracts other stallions from all over the area. Some of the admirers might be stronger than the stallion leading the band. The mare and the other members of the harem want to be sure that their band is led by the strongest and most powerful stallion around. If any of the new arrivals are able to take control of the band from the old stallion, the mares will mate with him. To keep this from happening, a stallion will put a lot of energy into defending his harem. Without any mares he will not be able to have any foals.

Young stallions that have left their bands often live together in small groups.

Two stallions fight for control of the band.

Time to Fight

When a new stallion approaches a band the leader tries to look as fierce as possible to scare the rival away. He flares his nostrils and opens his eyes wide. He prances toward the invader with his head held high and his neck arched. The rival does the same. The two horses snort and toss their heads and manes to persuade the other one to back down. They also stamp their hooves on the ground.

These tactics usually work. The weaker stallion realizes he cannot win a real fight and he heads off to look for another mare to mate with. But if the rival stallions are the same size they have to fight it out. They bite each other's neck and rear up on their hind legs to push their rival over with their forelegs. In the most fierce fights, the stallions spin around on their forelegs to deliver a mighty kick with their strong back legs.

New Arrival

After the fight the winning stallion mates with the harem. Eleven months later the foals are born. Wild horses give birth at night. The mare finds a place away from the band where she can give birth alone. That gives the mother and foal a chance to get to know each other before the foal meets the rest of the band.

At birth the foal is very weak and damp. The mother licks it dry and gently helps her baby to stand up for the first time. Most foals stand up before they are an hour old. But it takes a little longer before they can stand without wobbling.

A mare with her
newborn foal.

A young wild colt grazes with his mother and the rest of his band.

Welcome Foal

For a few hours the young horse is warmed by its mother's body and **nurses** on her milk. The young horse is then strong enough to join the band for the first time. The other horses crowd the new member, giving it welcoming sniffs and licks.

Within days the foal is trotting around. It jumps and kicks up its heels with the other young band members. After they have had fun playing with the other foals, the young horses need more milk from their mothers. Soon milk is not enough for the young horses and they begin to munch on grass and leaves. By the time they are three months old that is all they eat. By now the young horses are practicing the skills they will need as adults. The **colts**—young stallions— practice fighting. The **fillies**—young mares— learn to run faster and faster.

Mares will mate soon after givi... rse, sheep, deer, and
They produce one foal at ... mals.
filly or colt is three years...
or two younger brot... that have hair and feed
   At the age of ... ung with milk.
grown. It is ...
find a new ...
trouble with th ... ather, the stallion. He chases
his sons away to stop them from trying to mate
with his daughters. The young stallions search
for harems of their own. Most must wait until
they are much older before they are strong
enough to win one in a fight.

   Three-year-old fillies leave home as well.
They are now ready to mate. Some may join up
with a young stallion thrown out from another
band. Others join the harem of an older male.

Words to Know

...ly types of an existing species.

...f horses made up of a

...m of mares, and

Domestic horse	A horse that lives with people.
Evolved	Changed gradually over many generations to better suit the surroundings.
Feral	A description of a wild animal that is descended from a domestic animal.
Fillies	Young female horses.
Foals	Baby horses.
Habitats	Places where animals live.

Harem	A group of mares in a band.
Hoof	The foot of a ho[...] many other an[...]
Mammals	Animals [...] then yo[...]
Mares	Female horses.
Mate	To come together to produce young.
Molting	Shedding hair and growing new hair.
Mustangs	Wild horses living in North America.
Nurses	Drinks milk from a mother's body.
Predator	An animal that hunts other animals.
Species	The scientific word for animals of the same type that can breed together.
Stallion	A male horse.

Find Out More

Books

Ransford, S. *Horse and Pony Breeds*. Boston, Massachusetts: Kingfisher, 2003.

Stanley, G. E. *Wild Horses*. New York: Random House, 2007.

Web sites

Mustang
www.EnchantedLearning.com/subjects/mammals/horse/Mustangcoloring.shtml
Facts about mustangs with a picture to print and color in.

Mustangs Run Free WebQuest
eduscapes.com/nature/mustang/act.htm
A project for learning more about wild horses.

Index